CAREERS in Your Community™

WORKING in PUBLIC TRANSPORTATION

Mary-Lane Kamberg

Rosen YA
New York

For Rachel

Published in 2019 by The Rosen Publishing Group, Inc.
29 East 21st Street, New York, NY 10010

Copyright © 2019 by The Rosen Publishing Group, Inc.

First Edition

All rights reserved. No part of this book may be reproduced in any form without permission in writing from the publisher, except by a reviewer.

Library of Congress Cataloging-in-Publication Data

Names: Kamberg, Mary-Lane, 1948– author.
Title: Working in public transportation / Mary-Lane Kamberg.
Description: First edition. | New York : Rosen Publishing, 2019. | Series: Careers in your community | Includes bibliographical references and index. | Audience: Grades 7–12.
Identifiers: LCCN 2018010592 | ISBN 9781499467321 (library bound) | ISBN 9781499467406 (pbk.)
Subjects: LCSH: Transportation—United States—Juvenile literature. | Transportation—Vocational guidance—United States—Juvenile literature.
Classification: LCC HE203 .K36 2019 | DDC 388.023/73—dc23
LC record available at https://lccn.loc.gov/2018010592

Manufactured in the United States of America

Contents

Introduction	**4**
CHAPTER *One* **The Wheels on the Bus**	**7**
CHAPTER *Two* **All Aboard**	**19**
CHAPTER *Three* **The Lighter Side**	**30**
CHAPTER *Four* **Anchors Aweigh**	**41**
CHAPTER *Five* **Help Wanted**	**52**
Glossary	**65**
For More Information	**67**
For Further Reading	**71**
Bibliography	**73**
Index	**76**

Introduction

In urban areas everywhere, people are on the move. Heading to school, work, shops, and across town to visit a sick aunt, many of them use public transportation to get there. Buses, trains, light-rail, and ferries get people where they're going. These conveyances also offer job opportunities for those seeking careers in their communities.

For example, school bus and transit bus drivers play vital roles in getting students to school and adults to their workplaces. In congested cities buses keep passenger cars off the roads during the busy "drive time" when most people travel to and from work. The passengers depend on bus drivers to get them to school and work on time.

Commuter trains bring workers from suburbs into cities and back. Riders can enjoy "downtime" by relaxing, reading, or even putting in some extra work instead of battling traffic over what can be long distances, especially in places like Chicago and New York City.

Some public transportation workers operate subway or elevated trains with no separate locomotive, or electric-powered streetcar, trams, or trolleys to transport passengers over long or short distances leading in and out of cities or within city limits.

Introduction

Ferry operators let passengers cut across bodies of water to access destinations that would take much longer—or be impossible to reach—over land. Ferries transport vehicles as well as people along regular routes on which their communities depend.

Workers who operate subway trains and other forms of public transportation serve their communities by safely moving passengers from place to place.

WORKING in PUBLIC TRANSPORTATION

Each of these positions involves much more than getting passengers from one place to another. Keeping passengers safe is a major responsibility. In addition to knowing how to watch for potential hazards, workers in these careers may need to assist passengers with disabilities. These workers may also inspect equipment for needed maintenance or repair. In some cases, they run safety drills and perform other tasks.

Typical work days offer a great deal of independence. Instead of being stuck nine to five in an office, workers are out in the community in constant contact with the public. Personal qualities needed for these jobs include good people skills, like customer service, active listening, and communication. Other qualities include good observation and decision-making skills.

The occupations in the following sections require a high school diploma or the equivalent. Most workers need full physical abilities, including good vision and hearing. Some require additional skills in technology, and some need special licenses or certifications. On-the-job training is common.

In this book you'll learn in detail what these occupations involve to see if they sound like something you'd like to do. You'll also learn how to find job openings and get tips on applying and interviewing for them, as well as information about job outlook and ways to get ahead once you land the job.

CHAPTER One

The Wheels on the Bus

It's the first day of school and kids gather at neighborhood bus stops with book bags full of school supplies for the new year. A big, yellow bus pulls up. The driver opens the door and kids climb aboard. Across town, a transit bus driver pulls up to a stop. Men and women on their way to work, doctor

School bus drivers must learn traffic laws and routes, how to help children with disabilities, and how keep all passengers safe.

appointments, grocery stores, and more board the bus and pay the fare. They make their way to seats to ride to their destinations. School bus and transit bus drivers serve their communities by providing free or affordable transportation to and from important destinations.

American school districts annually spend an estimated $22 billion transporting twenty-five million children on ten billion student rides, according to the Amalgamated Transit Union (ATU), which represents school bus and transit bus drivers in the United States and Canada. About 55 percent of students in kindergarten through twelfth grade ride five hundred thousand school buses. The ATU is a labor union, an organization of workers that serves to improve member benefits and working conditions. Union representatives negotiate contracts with employers concerning such issues as wages, hours, fringe benefits, and job security. The Teamsters Union and the Transport Workers Union are other labor unions that represent workers in these occupations.

All in a Day's Work

School bus drivers are well trained. They spend part of summer reviewing traffic laws, practicing driving skills, and learning the routes to pick up students in the morning and safely return them after school. Depending on the size of the school district, drivers may make multiple runs for staggered start times for elementary, middle, and high schools. They may also transport sports teams and other groups to games, field trips, and other activities.

Along with picking up and dropping off passengers, school bus drivers follow a planned route on a

Unruly children can endanger other passengers by distracting the driver while in traffic. Drivers must maintain order and good behavior on the way to and from school.

specified time schedule. If needed, they assist small children and those with disabilities to get on and off the bus and cross streets. Drivers must maintain order and safety on the bus. They need to know the school system's rules and may have to report disciplinary problems to district supervisors or parents.

In addition to responsibility for passenger safety, including obeying traffic laws and regulations, they keep the bus clean. They often also check tires, brakes, windshield wipers, lights, fuel, and oil; perform other maintenance tasks; and report needed repairs. They may have to prepare reports about number of passengers, mileage, or fuel consumption for their employers.

Additional skills that may be needed include map reading and the use of mobile phones or two-way radios to report delays, accidents, or other situations.

GUINNESS WORLD RECORD HOLDER

When Carl Fisher retired from his job as school bus driver in Pleasant Hope, Missouri, in November 2012 at the age of eighty-two, he celebrated sixty-six years on the job. As of 2018 he was the Guinness World Record holder as the person with the "longest career as a bus driver." He began his career soon after his sixteenth birthday on December 12, 1946. His father, who drove the school bus before him, wanted more time to work the family farm. So Fisher took over the route. Since then he logged an estimated two million miles in more than twelve school buses, which he—not the school district—owned. Over the years he transported three generations of the same families. Before he retired, he was driving high school students to and from Ozark Technical College in nearby Springfield, Missouri.

All Through the Town

Like school bus drivers, local transit bus drivers follow a specific city or suburban route with frequent stops on a time schedule. According to the ATU, transit agencies annually provide more than twelve billion passenger trips in the United States and Canada. Although school bus drivers work only on school days, city bus drivers may work early mornings, late nights, and weekends. They may operate buses powered by gasoline, diesel, electricity, or compressed natural gas.

Driver responsibilities include ensuring passenger safety. They must obey traffic laws and other

Driving a city bus may be stressful during times of heavy traffic and bad weather. However, many drivers enjoy encountering members of the community.

regulations. They also assist older persons or those with disabilities when necessary.

Drivers regulate heating, lighting, and ventilation for passenger comfort. At times they must handle passenger emergencies. Transit drivers collect fares and answer questions about schedules, routes, and transfer points. Additional communication skills may be needed to calm unruly passengers or resolve conflicts. Drivers stay in touch with a central dispatcher to report delays, accidents, or traffic obstructions.

Tasks may include keeping the bus clean, as well as inspecting vehicles and checking for gas, oil, or water levels. Drivers may make such minor repairs as changing flat tires. They also record information about fares received and maintain a log book. Transit drivers need familiarity with such technology as internet browser software, operating system software like Microsoft Windows, and such map creation software as AOL MapQuest and Microsoft MapPoint.

Bus drivers have constant contact with students or members of the public. The job can be stressful due to heavy traffic or bad weather. According to the US Department of Labor, bus drivers have a higher rate of injuries and illnesses than the national average for all workers. Most injuries result from traffic accidents. However, the ATU says school buses are considered the safest motor vehicles on the road. The union reports that in the first decade of the twenty-first century only 0.34 percent of 370,000 fatal motor vehicle accidents were related to school transportation.

HOTEL CALIFORNIA?

It's after midnight in Silicon Valley, the nickname for the Santa Clara Valley in northern California. The going-home-from-work crowd has long ago departed. And it's hours too early for people to head back to the office. Yet the several buses winding their way along Santa Clara County Valley Transportation Authority's Route 22 are full of passengers: men, women, and children.

Most of them ride the entire two-hour, 35-mile (56 kilometer) route between Palo Alto and San Jose. Along the way they pass the local Microsoft office, as well as the headquarters of high-tech giants Google, Facebook, and Apple. At the end of the line, the passengers depart the bus. They wait about fifteen minutes and board another bus headed in the opposite direction.

Route 22 is the only 24-hour service in the area. And these late-night, early morning riders are among the estimated 7,394 homeless persons in San Jose/Santa Clara City/Santa Clara County, according to a 2017 report from the US Department of Housing and Urban Development. The area has the sixth-highest number of homeless persons in the United States.

For a one-way adult fare of $2.25, or an all-day pass for $7, these passengers have a safe place to sleep for the night. For $80, an adult can ride all month. Except for frequent stops along the way,

(continued on the next page)

(continued from the previous page)

passengers rest in relative comfort with a roof over their heads. The bus route has the nickname "Hotel 22." Valley Transit Authorities have no plans to interfere with these night riders. The agency does not discriminate against any riders as long as they pay the fare and obey the no smoking, no eating, and no drinking rules.

Education and Training Requirements

Personal characteristics best suited to bus drivers include patience, problem-solving, critical thinking, and good decision-making skills. Other helpful skills include customer service, observation, active listening, and time management.

Bus drivers need good physical health and strength, including normal use of arms and legs, hand-eye coordination, and good hearing and vision. Some specific health issues disqualify an applicant. These include high blood pressure, epilepsy, Meniere's disease, and others. Most states require drivers to be at least eighteen years of age, and many require fluent English.

States regulate bus drivers within their borders. Federal regulations apply to buses that cross state lines. In most states, drivers must have a high school diploma or equivalent and one to three months of training that includes driving and classroom instruction.

During driving training, new hires first drive the bus on a closed course. Once they successfully pass that section, they move on to driving in light traffic. They then practice the route. Finally, they drive with passengers along with an experienced driver. The experienced driver coaches them along the way and also evaluates their performances.

Classroom instruction includes information about company rules and regulations and state and municipal traffic laws. Instructors cover schedules, routes, fares, and safe driving practices. Additional topics may include first-aid procedures, as well as tips on how to interact with passengers.

Bus drivers need a Class B commercial driver's license (CDL). They can earn the CDL before being hired. Or, in some cases, they can qualify for it during on-the-job training. Qualifications vary by state, but generally include both written and driving tests. However, a CDL is not enough.

All bus drivers must also pass additional written and road driving tests to get a passenger endorsement, or P endorsement. The P endorsement is an additional certification that shows that the driver is qualified to drive vehicles that hold at least sixteen passengers. It is similar to the endorsement on a driver's license that shows that the driver can legally operate a motorcycle.

A driver with a P endorsement has passed a knowledge test that covers the following topics:
- Safe loading and unloading of passengers
- Operating push-out window emergency exits
- Accidents
- Fires
- Interactions with hostile or troublesome passengers

WORKING in PUBLIC TRANSPORTATION

Bus drivers need specialized driver's licenses that show they have passed tests of their knowledge and driving abilities before they get behind the wheel of a bus.

The Wheels on the Bus

- Defensive driving
- Braking
- Proper action concerning railroad crossings and drawbridges

Along with a P endorsement, school bus drivers need a school bus (S) endorsement. An S endorsement shows that the driver has passed extra requirements to operate a school bus, including additional written and driving tests. The written exam for the S endorsement covers such subjects as:

- Safe loading and unloading of children
- Operation of such safety devices as stop signals, external mirrors, flashing lights, warning devices, and other safety equipment
- Procedures for using emergency exits and evacuations
- Proper action concerning railroad crossings
- Handling emergency situations
- Safe vehicle operation
- Defensive driving techniques

Practice tests for both of these exams are available online.

The road skills test for both kinds of bus drivers covers pre-trip inspection, vehicle control, and driving on the road. Bus driver applicants must pass a background check. Some states require a physical exam every two years, as well as random drug and alcohol testing while on duty.

The Road Ahead

Overall employment of bus drivers in the United States is projected to grow 6 percent from 2016 to 2026, according to the US Bureau of Labor Statistics. That rate is about the same as the average for all occupations. Because of driver turnover, job openings will exist, especially for applicants willing to work part-time or irregular shifts.

Also, according to the US Bureau of Labor Statistics, opportunities for school bus drivers are expected to grow 5 percent between 2016 and 2026, largely because of an increase in the number of school-age children. Employment of city bus drivers is projected to grow 9 percent in the same period.

CHAPTER *Two*

All Aboard

On weekdays Roy boards a commuter train at a station in Des Plaines, Illinois, and rides about thirty minutes into the city of Chicago for work. At the end of the day, he reverses his route to go home. Instead of fighting car traffic, Roy can read a newspaper, check his email, prepare for his day, or just relax. The alternative is driving his own car. However, if everyone who rides commuter rail into Chicago drove a car instead, the roads couldn't

Commuter rails help minimize the number of cars on the road. Plus, passengers can relax on the way to work instead of fighting traffic.

handle the traffic. Neither could the already challenged parking lot space.

Commuter rail appeals to those riders who want to avoid traffic congestion. Others like it for such environmental reasons as reducing their dependence on fossil fuels. In addition, many riders prefer using public transportation instead of incurring the rising costs of owning, insuring, driving, and parking their own cars and trucks.

Commuter rail is also known as suburban rail. It's a passenger service that runs along railway tracks between outer suburbs and a central business district. The service has scheduled, fixed routes. Its target market includes riders who travel daily to and from jobs at the same destinations. Many commuter trains run only during the morning and evening "rush" periods when most people go to work or return home.

Typically, commuter trains use passenger cars that are either self-propelled or pulled by diesel-electric or electric locomotives. In some cities the trains use electric power from either a third rail or, particularly in the northeastern United States, a catenary wire. Catenary wire is a system of overhead wires. The system allows faster acceleration, as well as lower noise levels and reduced negative air quality effects.

Chugging Along

Workers in commuter rail occupations serve their communities by providing dependable, convenient transportation for large numbers of people who live in suburbs and work in major cities. Locomotive engineers and conductors are the two main jobs in commuter train operations. Engineers drive the

All Aboard

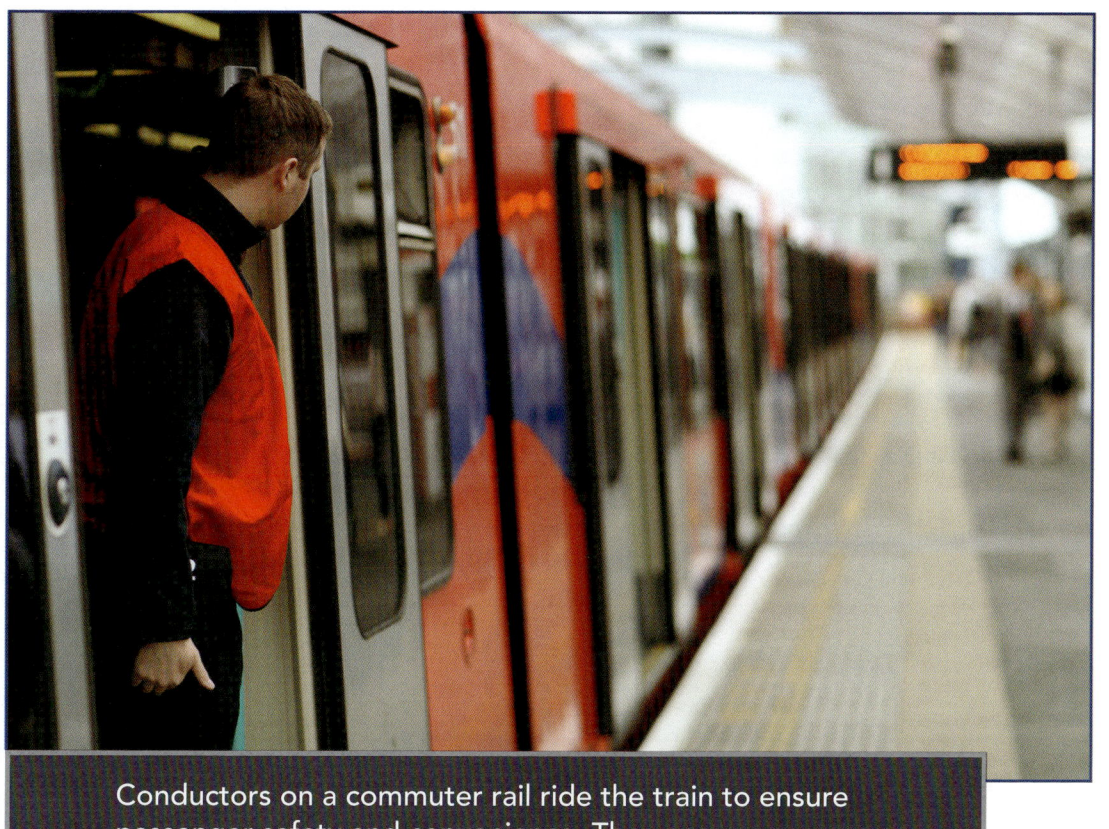

Conductors on a commuter rail ride the train to ensure passenger safety and convenience. They answer passenger questions and sell tickets when needed.

trains. Conductors ride them to ensure passenger safety and comfort. They both usually work predictable, full-time schedules. However, some engineers and conductors work as "extra board," temporary substitute workers. Engineers and conductors with the most seniority get the most desired shifts. Seniority refers to the time the worker has served on the job compared to other employees.

Conductors tell engineers when to start the train. Conductors ride the train and oversee crew activities. Their main role is to ensure safety and orderly passenger behavior. They respond to upset or unruly passengers. In emergencies conductors help passengers get to safety.

Conductors also check previously purchased tickets and sell tickets to passengers who need them. As trains approach stations, conductors announce the stops. They make additional announcements as needed to keep passengers informed.

Engineers operate the locomotives. Most locomotive engineers first work as conductors for several years. The engines they drive may be electric; diesel-electric; or powered by battery, steam, or gas-turbine electricity. Engineers use such controls as throttles and airbrakes to operate the train. They follow safety procedures, as well as railroad rules and regulations.

While driving the train, they monitor gauges, dials, and other instruments for speed, battery charge, air pressure in brake lines, and other information. They also watch the track for obstacles and respond to emergencies or breakdowns. If delays or changes in schedules occur, they use two-way radios to talk with dispatchers.

Before each run engineers check fuel, water, and other necessary supplies. Their responsibilities also include checks and adjustments of the mechanical condition of the locomotives. After the run engineers inspect the locomotives looking for damaged or defective equipment.

Documentation is another aspect of the job. Engineers must report mechanical issues that need additional inspection. They make sure procedural manuals and logbooks are available in the cab of the train. They also communicate about such problems as accidents, signaling problems, unscheduled stops, and delays.

DON'T TEXT AND DRIVE

Texting while driving a train caused a commuter train accident in 2008. The crash killed twenty-five and injured one hundred passengers and crew in Chatsworth, California, near Los Angeles, according to news network CNN.

In the late afternoon of September 12, 2008, the engineer of a Metrolink commuter train was texting on a mobile phone. The National Transportation Safety Board said the distraction made him miss a red signal and fail to stop.

The three-passenger-car train then crashed head-on into a seventeen-car Union Pacific freight train. The engineer was among the dead. The train locomotive and one of the passenger cars derailed. On the freight train, two locomotives and ten cars left the track.

Metrolink had rules in place against using wireless devices while operating trains. The NTSB said the commuter train had no positive train control (PTC) technology. Positive train control is a set of technologies that includes global positioning systems (GPS). PTC monitors trains and stops them before colliding, derailing due to speeding, and other preventable movement.

After the Chatsworth accident, the Rail Safety Improvement Act of 2008 required all passenger railroads and Class I freight railroads to install PTC on main lines used to transport passengers or hazardous materials by the end of 2020.

On the Right Track

Commuter rail workers need good leadership, decision-making, customer service, and oral and written communication skills. They also need physical abilities that include good hearing and vision, including telling colors apart. Good manual dexterity, hand-eye coordination, and reaction time also are important. Applicants must be at least eighteen years of age and have a valid motor vehicle driver's license. Previous work experience that includes working on an on-call basis or varying shift schedules is helpful.

Applicants need a high school diploma or equivalent. They must pass a background check, as well as a check of their motor vehicle records. And they're subject to random drug and alcohol screenings while on the job.

Technology use also is important. These occupations require familiarity with the following types of software:
- Database user and query (data entry)
- Electric train management systems (ETMS) or positive train control systems (PTC)
- Route navigation (route mapping)
- Spreadsheet (Microsoft Excel)
- Time accounting (time tracking)
- Work processing (Microsoft Word)

Conducting Business

Conductors on commuter railroads must be certified through a training program approved by the Federal Railroad Administration. Some operators, like Amtrak, provide their own training programs. Some others may use a central training facility or community

All Aboard

Crowded conditions may make some riders angry or frustrated. Conductors are trained to deal with disruptive passengers if necessary.

college. Conductors learn such skills as ticketing procedures and how to serve passengers, as well as how to handle those who are angry or unruly.

Applicants may consider earning an associate's degree through a community college. Programs may include railroad operations, railroad conductor technology, or conductor training. These courses of study often include such topics as railroad history, operations rules, and conductor duties. The programs combine classroom study and internships. An internship is a temporary paid or unpaid job that provides practical work experience.

One such program is the National Academy of Railroad Sciences, a partnership between Johnson County Community College in Overland Park, Kansas, and the BNSF Railway. The hands-on program in laboratory conditions includes railroad safety training. Conductors also need one to three months of on-the-job training.

Over the course of their employment, conductors must complete additional training concerning changes in operating rules, operating practices, new federal regulations, and new equipment in service. Some conductors advance to locomotive engineers after several years' experience.

Driving the Train

Applicants for locomotive engineer openings must be at least twenty-one years of age. Like conductors, engineers must be certified by the Federal Railroad Administration. Certification involves a written knowledge test, a skills test, and a supervisor's determination that the engineer knows all aspects of the route where he or she will work. This knowledge includes track length, position of switches, and features of the track.

Engineers must pass vision, hearing, and medical exams. They also need two to three months of on-the-job training before they can operate a train on their own. The practical training involves riding with an

All Aboard

The Federal Railroad Administration must certify that an engineer has passed written and driving tests, as well as demonstrated knowledge of his or her route.

experienced engineer who is familiar with the route. During their careers, engineers must maintain skills through continuing education. Certification must be renewed every three years.

According to the US Department of Labor, in 2016 most railroad workers belonged to a labor union. Unions negotiate contracts with employers for union members. Such unions as the Commuter Rail Employees Union, Amalgamated Transit Union, the United Transportation Union, and the Brotherhood of Locomotive Engineers and Trainmen represent workers in these occupations.

WORKING in PUBLIC TRANSPORTATION

TROUBLE ON THE TRACKS

In 2013 officials of the Massachusetts Bay Transit Authority (MBTA) knew they had a problem. They ran the sixth-largest commuter rail system in the United States, according to the National Transit Database. However, its annual thirty-five million passenger trips represented a 13 percent decline from forty million ten years earlier. Over the same period the national average ridership increased 63 percent. The MBTA was the only commuter railway in the country that wasn't growing—even though the Greater Boston population was.

The trains were often late—as much as a half hour. Passengers complained that toilets were dirty, and the heaters and air conditioners didn't work. The average fare had more than doubled over the decade. Operations costs were high, and the system was $5 million in debt, according to the Pioneer Institute, a Boston-based think tank.

On July 1, 2014, the Massachusetts Department of Transportation hired Keolis to operate the network. The French rail company replaced the Massachusetts Bay Commuter Rail Company, which had run the commuter service since 2003.

By 2016 MDTA had invested $100 million to improve service. New seats and communications equipment were installed. And Keolis was using drones to inspect bridges and look for downed trees and other obstructions on tracks to avoid delays. Although some of the lines still had lateness issues, the commuter service boasted an overall on-time rate of 89 percent, according to MDTA.

Down the Line

Overall employment in railroad occupations in the United States is expected to decline 3 percent between 2016 and 2026, according to the US Department of Labor. However, the decline is expected among workers on freight trains, not commuter rail. Demand for freight transportation of such bulk commodities as oil is expected to be replaced by the use of pipelines. The reduced use of coal in favor of natural gas to produce electricity may also lessen demand for freight train workers.

However, locomotive engineers and conductors are increasingly replacing locomotive firers. Locomotive firers are sometimes part of a train crew. They monitor train instruments and watch for obstacles on the tracks and other potential safety problems. Employment in that role is expected to decline 79 percent between 2016 and 2026. Some of these tasks have become automated. In other cases, these tasks are performed by locomotive engineers or conductors. In addition, many job openings will result from the need to replace engineers and conductors who retire.

CHAPTER *Three*

The Lighter Side

Some public transit systems fall into the category of light-rail. Like other types of public transportation, light-rail reduces traffic congestion in big cities where large numbers of people are going places. Light-rail includes streetcars, elevated trains, and some subways. Most light-rail consists of one to four rail cars.

The cars have a lighter frame and smaller body than their "heavy rail" cousins. Some light-rail trains use diesel fuel. However, most use electric power from either overhead wires or a "live" third rail beside the track. Typical light-rail routes run between 5 and 15 miles (8 and 24 km) long.

Neither streetcars nor light-rail trains share track with "heavy rail" passenger or freight trains. Light-rail runs on two types of track. Streetcars—sometimes called trolleys—use track laid in city streets. These vehicles share the roads with motor vehicles and buses. Operators must obey such traffic laws as stopping for red lights. Subways run underground for all or part of their routes. Elevated trains run on track built above other roadways. Both use their own tracks in their own right of way. Right of way is a legal right to pass along a specific route.

The Lighter Side

Track for streetcars is laid into city streets, where these light-rail conveyances share the road with buses and motor vehicles. Drivers must obey traffic laws.

WORKING in PUBLIC TRANSPORTATION

Light-Rail Occupations

Communities need light-rail and streetcar operators to drive rail-guided public transportation. Drivers operate controls to open and close vehicle doors at each stop. They must safely regulate speed as well as time spent at each stop. They also direct emergency evacuation action plans. Job responsibilities include staying alert to potential obstructions and hazards.

Light-rail operators typically work more than forty hours per week seated in an enclosed vehicle. They may be asked to work early mornings, late nights, weekends, and holidays. They have constant contact

Light-rail operators don't steer the train, but they do control acceleration and braking. They also control how long the train waits at each stop.

with their work group, as well as customers. Some riders can be unpleasant or even angry and unruly. Operators use intercom and public address systems to communicate with passengers.

Drivers greet passengers and answer questions about fares, schedules, transfers, and routes. They also make announcements such as for upcoming stops or schedule delays. Some operators collect fares, although this task is increasingly becoming automated. Operators' duties include reporting fares collected, shift summaries, and any incidents or accidents. Operators must report any delays, mechanical problems, or emergencies to dispatchers or supervisors, usually by radio.

Because the cars run on tracks, there's no need to steer. Instead, an operator's most important control is a lever that either moves the train forward or makes it stop. If the operator lets go of the lever, a "dead man's pedal" automatically activates. A dead man's pedal is an electrical switch that slows or stops the train if the operator of a train lets go. Its name comes from the idea that if an operator dies, loses consciousness, or is physically removed from control, the train and its passengers remain safe. Operators also use such equipment as track switches, braking systems, defrosting systems, horns, bells, whistle pulls, and wheelchair ramps.

Early Beginnings

The idea of light-rail in North America dates to the 1960s when the city of San Francisco, California, was building its Bay Area Rapid Transit system known as BART. BART is a heavy rail public transportation

WORKING in PUBLIC TRANSPORTATION

service that connects the city to outlying counties. In the planning stages, officials decided to use a light-rail system in a BART tunnel then being built on Market Street.

Planners ordered one hundred Standard Light-Rail Vehicles (SLRV) from Boeing Vertol. The tunnel was completed in 1978. The first cars arrived in 1979, and the Muni Metro began operations on February 18, 1980.

Unfortunately, the Boeing Vertol cars failed to live up to expectations. Doors jammed, roofs leaked, and brakes and motors proved defective. Frequent breakdowns and accidents were the result. In 1998 the railway began trading out the cars for new ones. These new cars, manufactured by the AnsaldoBreda engineering company based in Italy, also were unsatisfactory. They screeched during acceleration and braking. They caused underground vibrations that worried owners of properties along the routes. The cars were difficult to couple together so trains had fewer cars. Coupling is a method of connecting rail cars together. That limited the trains' passenger capacity. When the time came to replace the Breda cars, the company was disqualified from even submitting a bid.

New Cars

The need for new cars resulted from the Breda cars reaching their twenty-five-year life expectancy, along with the need for more capacity. Additional cars will be used for the city's new Central Subway, which is due for completion in 2019. The authority plans to replace its entire fleet between 2021 and 2040 with S200 class cars from Siemens, a global automation company headquartered in Germany. The model can

The Lighter Side

San Francisco, California's, Muni Metro public transportation system is a direct descendant of the historic horse-drawn trolleys that once operated there.

couple up to five cars, increasing potential ridership per train. The first of the new cars began service in 2017.

Today the Muni Metro is a light-rail system directly descended from the city's historic horse-drawn streetcars. The San Francisco Municipal Railway operates it on a variety of rights of way. It runs through tunnels, on the surface, and along streetcar sections in mixed traffic. Passengers board and depart at both high-platform stations and traditional curbside streetcar stops.

Along with San Francisco, other North American cities developed their own light-rail systems beginning around the same time. They are in use by commuters and tourists in such cities as Calgary in Alberta, Canada (the C-Train); Portland, Oregon (the Metropolitan Area Express); St. Louis, Missouri (the MetroLink); Sacramento, California (the Sacramento Regional Transit District System); San Diego, California (the San Diego Trolley), and others.

Being Neighborly

Many American cities also use streetcars on rails to connect restaurants, offices, and pedestrian areas in order to create urban "walkable" neighborhoods. An example of such a streetcar system is the KC Streetcar Project in Kansas City, Missouri. Its 2-mile (3.2 km), north-south route has sixteen stops two blocks apart on Main Street in the heart of the city's business district. It runs seven days a week during limited hours.

The system is operated by the KC Streetcar Authority. Passengers pay no fares. They typically ride the streetcar to patronize businesses, hotels, restaurants, art galleries, educational facilities, and neighborhoods. The stops include such attractions as the River Market, the Kansas City Public Library, the Power and Light entertainment area, Union Station, and others.

Traits and Training

Applicants for light-rail occupations need a high school diploma or the equivalent and a valid driver's license with a clean driving record. Most employers require the applicant to be at least twenty-one years of age. Applicants need good decision-making and

The Lighter Side

RECORD-BREAKING STREETCAR

As of 2018, a light-rail streetcar manufactured by the Mobility Division of the Siemens Corporation held the Guinness World Record for the longest distance traveled by a battery-powered streetcar from one charge. The Siemens S70 light-rail vehicle traveled 15.283 miles (24.596 km) in twenty-four hours in July 2014. The car was designed with cooperation from a Siemen's customer, the Metropolitan Transit System's Green Line in San Diego, California.

The S70 has a modular design that can be adapted for both streetcars and light-rail vehicles. It has a top speed of 35 miles (56 km) per hour. It can also be modified for use with a variety of overhead power supplies. The light-rail cars are 9 feet (2.7 meters) longer than the streetcar versions. Seats in the streetcar face the doors. Those in the light-rail version face the cab. Most S70s have controls at both ends and doors on both sides, although some transit agencies order different characteristics.

customer service skills. Experience in any customer service job is helpful.

Successful candidates must be able to work independently. They should be able to handle stressful situations with tact, patience, and courtesy.

They also need the ability to communicate. Some employers require fluent English. Manual dexterity is necessary to handle controls and tools in repetitive motions. Candidates with one or more years' experience as truck, school bus, or transit bus drivers are preferred. Medical exams, drug testing, and background checks are usually required.

On-the-job training is provided by employers. The instruction, which lasts several months, includes both classroom work and field training. Classroom work involves safety training, operating rules, and other topics. Field training involves operating various types of equipment.

For example, the Santa Clara Valley Transportation Authority issues a seventeen-page rule book trainees must understand and follow. Topics include passenger assistance, public relations, dealing with hazardous materials, and what to do when a person is on the right of way. It also covers rules about speed and backing up. Operators must learn hand signals for stop and stay, reduce speed, proceed, and back up, as well as flag, bell, and horn signals.

Field training is accomplished under the supervision of a technical trainer, transportation supervisor, line instructor, or qualified operator. Trainees must pass both written and practical tests. Sometimes seasoned veterans take refresher courses.

A Parallel Universe

Some training programs use railroad simulators to hone trainees' skills before they operate the real thing. A simulator is a machine or piece of equipment used for training purposes that imitates the environment and

The Lighter Side

conditions of an actual event. It creates an almost-real experience such as operating a train.

For example, the Regional Transportation District (RTD) in Denver, Colorado, purchased a $1.5 million simulator to train about two hundred fifty operators, supervisors, and other employees annually. The simulator was manufactured by Oktal Simulation, based in Toulouse, France. Its console looks like what the operators will use on a real train. And the routes trainees see are duplicates of actual RTD routes. Trainees feel the bumps and stops along the routes. They'll experience the same G-forces and the senses of the train moving forward, braking, and going up and down hills. The screen can also reflect every weather condition an operator might face in the Denver area. Trainees may also deal with unexpected potential hazards.

Use of the simulator improves safety. If a trainee makes a mistake, no people or property are in danger. The simulator also saves costs by producing controlled conditions in the RTD's training facility. The company no longer has to take vehicles off the tracks for training.

Getting Ahead

Many light-rail operators work as part-time or temporary employees when they're first hired. Full-time openings go to those with the most seniority. Seniority also affects when an operator can choose his or her route or work schedule. Some operators move into dispatch, training, supervising, or management roles.

Wage increases and other benefits usually depend on contracts negotiated between labor unions and employers. The Amalgamated Transit Union represents

WORKING in PUBLIC TRANSPORTATION

Bay Area Rapid Transit system employees represented by the Amalgamated Transit Union in San Francisco picketed in 2013, demanding wage increases and other benefits.

light-rail, subway, and streetcar operators, as well as workers in other occupations.

Employment in light-rail occupations is expected to grow between 2 and 4 percent between 2016 and 2026, according to O-Net online, a service sponsored by the US Department of Labor. This rate is slower than the average growth for all occupations. The slow growth is due in part to the fact that many light-rail trains are now automated and need no operators at all.

CHAPTER *Four*

Anchors Aweigh

Vincent "Vinny" Lombardi couldn't believe his eyes. On the afternoon of January 15, 2009, just an hour into his shift, he stood at the helm of the NY Waterway ferryboat *Thomas Jefferson,* transporting

The commuter ferry *Thomas Jefferson* was the first rescue vessel to reach the United Airlines Airbus when it "landed" on the Hudson River in 2009.

thirty-one commuters. He watched an Airbus A320 "land" on the Hudson River.

Because his ferry created only a small wake, Lombardi knew he could get close to the plane without swamping the passengers, who were crawling out onto the wings. Although the plane remained afloat, the wings were covered in ankle-deep, 39-degree Fahrenheit (4-degree Celsius) water. It was the coldest day of the winter to that point, with an air temperature of 21°F (–6°C) and a wind chill of 11°F (–12°C).

The Airbus operated by United Airlines as Flight 1549 had taken off from New York's LaGuardia Airport headed for Charlotte, North Carolina. It carried 150 passengers and five crew members. Just three minutes later the plane ran into a flock of Canada geese. Incredibly, birds struck both of the plane's CFM56-5B engines. The engines failed, leaving the plane powerless at an altitude of 3,000 feet (914 m).

Just four minutes after the emergency landing that became known as "The Miracle on the Hudson," the *Thomas Jefferson* was the first vessel to reach the plane. Lombardi used his boat's rescue platform, and survivors walked across it to board the ferry. Crew members took off their own lifejackets and asked the commuters to follow suit. Deckhands and commuters formed a line and passed the jackets to survivors standing on the wing. Fifty-six of them climbed aboard the ferry.

Other commercial ferries soon joined Lombardi's. So did police, fire, and US Coast Guard boats. The *Thomas Jefferson* captain headed back to shore where

EMS crews in New York ambulances waited to treat survivors, who had only minor injuries and hypothermia. (Hypothermia is a medical condition of dangerously low body temperature.) The captain also told his crew to count the survivors and list their names. He knew authorities would want to know whether all airline passengers were accounted for.

Lombardi was well trained to handle the rescue mission. The captain first joined NY Waterway in 2001 as an armed security guard. But his passion was boating. Even in high school he dreamed of a career on the water. Later he wanted to run a charter fishing boat. Soon after taking the security job, he asked if he could become a deckhand instead. He took courses at a maritime academy. In 2003 he earned a promotion to captain. Lombardi plays himself in director Clint Eastwood's 2016 motion picture *Sully* about the events of that day.

Not every commuter ferry captain has to rescue airline passengers from a floating plane. But all of them are responsible for the safety of their passengers and crew.

Aye, Aye, Captain

Water transportation workers are also known as merchant mariners. Merchant mariners include ferry captains and deckhands, who operate and maintain nonmilitary boats. Those who work on ferries move people and vehicles over coastal and inland waterways, as well as other navigable water, such as the Great Lakes. They serve their communities by providing water transportation that shortens the time

WORKING in PUBLIC TRANSPORTATION

Ferry captains and deckhands face the same weather conditions as mariners on the ocean. However, the shorter trips mean ferry workers go home each night.

and distance necessary for an over-the-road route. Ferries also provide service to islands accessible only by air or sea.

Captains, sometimes called masters, assume overall command of the ferry. Captains steer the boats. They need knowledge of local weather and the ability to adjust navigation to conditions. They dock and undock the boats and supervise loading and discharging of passengers. They ensure passenger safety by following proper procedures. They also conduct quarterly emergency drills for such events as fire, man overboard, abandon ship, and security threats.

During regularly scheduled runs, captains read gauges to monitor levels of hydraulic fluid, air pressure, or oxygen. They use radios, depth finders, radar, lights, or buoys. They may use whistles, flashing lights, flags, or radios to signal other vessels moving on the water.

Captains inspect their vessels and equipment to ensure compliance with regulations. They're also responsible for maintaining the ferry, as well as such equipment as engines, winches, navigational systems, fire extinguishers, and life preservers. They may arrange for fuel, supplies, and repairs.

Ferry captains need good written communication skills to keep accurate records. They must log daily activities and safety drills. They must also fill out personnel reports and log weather and water conditions and pollution control activities.

Give Me a Hand

In addition to the captain, most ferries need one or more deckhands. Deckhands are sometimes called sailors or seamen. Entry-level deckhands are known as ordinary seamen. They perform the easiest tasks. Deckhands with experience are called able seamen.

All deckhands must follow the vessel's strict chain of command and obey captain's orders. They operate and maintain deck equipment other than the engine and motor. Deckhands also rig tow lines, open and close gates or ramps, and pull guard chains across entry points. They may also collect fares from passengers.

Ferry workers are usually away for only a few hours at a time. Like all mariners they're exposed to all kinds of weather. Unlike their seafaring counterparts, however, ferry captains and deckhands return home each night.

Ferry captains and deckhands need to know how to use a variety of computer software. Examples include the following:
- Autodesk Revit, computer-aided design (CAD) software
- KNMI TurboWin, database user interface and query software
- K-Log, log book software
- THINKmarine, computerized maintenance management system (CMMS)
- Microsoft Office suite

TRACING ANCESTRY

Perhaps the most famous ferryboat in the United States is the Staten Island Ferry. It carries passengers across the New York Harbor on twenty-five-minute, 5.2-mile (8.4-km) trips. Passengers enjoy views of the Statue of Liberty, Ellis Island, and the Manhattan skyline. The ferry route annually makes more than twenty-three million passenger trips, according to marketing organization NYC & Company.

The New York City Department of Transportation operates its nine vessels. They run twenty-four hours per day, 365 days per year. During weekday rush hours, five boats leave fifteen minutes apart. Four boats operate on weekends.

The Staten Island Ferry is a direct descendent of New York's first mechanical ferry system operated by the Richmond Turnpike Company in 1817. At the time, no bridges connected the areas that later became the city's boroughs. So water transportation was important. A borough is a division of a city. New York City's five boroughs include Manhattan, the Bronx, Queens, Brooklyn, and Staten Island.

As Staten Island grew, so did the route's traffic. When the Staten Island Railway began operations in 1860, ridership grew even more. The turnpike company sold its ferry holdings to the Baltimore and Ohio Railroad in 1884. The railroad used the Staten Island Rapid Transit Railroad to operate the route.

(continued on the next page)

WORKING in PUBLIC TRANSPORTATION

(continued from the previous page)

On June 14, 1901, its ferry *Northfield* sank after a collision with another vessel. Five of the 995 passengers aboard were missing and presumed drowned. The accident prompted New York City leaders to take over the ferry service under its Department of Docks and Ferries. The department purchased five new ferries named after each of the city's boroughs. In 1905 the *Manhattan* was the first to run as the Staten Island Ferry. The route has used the name ever since.

When the Staten Island Ferry docks at the St. George Terminal, a worker positions a ferry ramp so passengers and vehicles can go ashore.

Learning the Ropes

Entry-level deckhands have no educational requirements. They need on-the-job training for six months to a year. However, some employers may prefer to hire workers who have earned a bachelor's degree from a merchant marine academy.

Potential workers need good customer service and mechanical skills. They need manual dexterity and hand-eye coordination. They must also pass vision and hearing tests. Most water transportation jobs require the Transportation Worker Identification Credential from the Transportation Security Administration. This credential must be renewed every five years.

In addition, they need the Merchant Mariner Credential from the US Coast Guard. This credential also requires five-year renewals, as well as physical examinations every five years. Applicants must be American citizens or permanent US residents. They must pass a security screening and attend a class on shipboard safety. They are subject to preemployment drug testing, random drug and alcohol testing when on duty, and required drug and alcohol testing in the event of an accident.

Captains must be licensed by the US Coast Guard after rigorous training and boating experience. Licensing depends on a criminal background check and National Driver's Registry Report, as well as current first aid and cardiopulmonary resuscitation (CPR) certificates.

WORKING in PUBLIC TRANSPORTATION

Sailing Away

Work experience is an important factor for merchant mariners' advancement from lower-level to higher-level jobs. Another way to get ahead is to earn additional endorsements on the Merchant Mariner Credential. For example, to advance from ordinary seaman to unlimited able seaman usually takes three years' experience. However, after six to twelve months' experience, an ordinary seaman can earn endorsements that allow him or her to perform additional tasks, depending on the type of vessel on which he or she works.

A variety of labor unions represent workers in merchant mariner occupations. These include the

On-the-job training gives merchant mariners the skills and experience they need to work as captains or deckhands on transit ferries.

Amalgamated Transit Union, Seafarers International Union, Sailors' Union of the Pacific, American Maritime Officers, Inland Boatmen's Union, the Maritime Union, and the International Organization of Masters, Mates & Pilots.

Job openings should be favorable for most water transportation workers. Required licenses, certifications, and security qualifications may discourage potential employees, thus reducing the competition for these jobs. According to the US Department of Labor, overall employment of water transportation workers is projected to grow 8 percent between 2016 and 2026, about as fast as the average for all occupations. Growth is expected because of the US Department of Transportation's Maritime Administration's Marine Highways initiatives to develop and expand freight and passenger water transportation.

CHAPTER Five

Help Wanted

The outlook for jobs in public transportation varies by each occupation. So does the range of pay you can expect. For current information about pay for transit workers, visit the US Bureau of Labor Statistics website.

If you think one of these occupations is for you, you can begin preparing while you're still in high school. Choose classes and extracurricular activities that will make your résumé stand out. A résumé is a document that lists a job applicant's education, work experience, and other qualifications. Job seekers use it together with the employer's application form in hopes of being called in for an interview. An interview usually is a face-to-face meeting between an applicant and a representative of the employer. Sometimes initial job interviews are conducted by telephone or over the internet. However, at some point most employers want to meet desired candidates in person.

To build your education and other qualifications, become familiar with what public transit employers seek. Because good verbal and written skills are important in these occupations, take classes in English composition and speech. And because technology continues to grow in importance in these fields, take as many computer classes as you can. The more experience you have with computer technology, the easier you'll be able to learn new software employers adopt in the future.

Help Wanted

At some point in the hiring process employers want to meet applicants for public transit jobs face to face to determine if they're suited for the opening.

Learn a foreign language that is common among ethnic populations in the employer's service area. Consider learning American Sign Language (ASL) to communicate with passengers who have hearing disabilities. ASL is an unspoken language that uses hand and finger gestures, movements, and facial expressions to convey meaning. In addition, participate in high school clubs and sports teams to build teamwork and leadership skills. These skills come in handy when dealing with the public in a customer service role.

WORKING in PUBLIC TRANSPORTATION

If you work during the school year or summer, look for a job that involves customer service, public safety, good communication, or other desired skills. Once you enter the full-time workforce, seek jobs where you'll get the kinds of experience employers look for. Work experience using the skills transit workers need is always a plus in the job application process. So is extra training. Take first aid and CPR courses at a local hospital or community center. You may have to get certified again. But the fact that you took the classes shows your interest in public safety.

While you're doing all that, drive carefully! Many public transit employers look back three years or more at an applicant's motor vehicle driving record. A long list of tickets and accidents will likely move a person's application to the bottom of the pile—or the wastebasket.

QUESTIONS AND ANSWERS

Many public transportation jobs require special licenses or certifications. For example, bus drivers need a commercial driver's license. Earning one involves both practical and written tests. All questions on the written test are multiple choice with four possible answers. The test takers may be asked to complete a sentence, answer a question, choose the best answer, or fill in the blank. Here are some examples of the kinds of questions on the written tests:

1. While driving a bus, where should you be looking?
    a. To the left
    b. To the right
    c. Straight ahead close to the bus
    d. Back and forth, near and far

2. If your bus hydroplanes, what should you do?
    a. Speed up
    b. Release the gas pedal
    c. Counter steer
    d. Pump the brakes

3. Which of the following should you know when crossing traffic in a heavy vehicle?
    a. A heavy vehicle is easy to see, so other drivers will slow down or get out of your way.
    b. Heavy vehicles need longer spaces between traffic than cars.
    c. The lighter the load, the more space a heavy vehicle needs to cross traffic.
    d. Pulling halfway across and blocking one lane, while waiting for traffic coming from the opposite direction to clear, is the safest way to cross traffic.

4. If air pressure drops in the service air tanks, a heavy vehicle driver must be able to see a warning before it drops below _____ psi.
    a. 30
    b. 50
    c. 60
    d. 100

(continued on the next page)

WORKING in PUBLIC TRANSPORTATION

(continued from the previous page)

To prepare for public transportation certification or licensing exams, look for books of practice tests and tips for taking them. You can borrow them at your local library and through interlibrary loan. You can also purchase the materials online and in bookstores. Be sure to get the most recent editions available.

Answers: 1D, 2B, 3B, 4C

Showing Off

Before applying for public transportation jobs, create a résumé that shows you in the best possible light. Everything you list should contribute to the conclusion that you are the best possible candidate. This is definitely not the place to be humble! At the same time, everything on a résumé must be true and accurate. Many employers fire workers who are found lying on their applications, even if the workers are doing a good job.

To compose the best résumé, seek advice from books, magazine articles, and résumé-building websites. You'll find tips about what to include and how to present it. You'll also be able to see several sample résumés after which you can model yours. Some free résumé-building sites include the following:

Help Wanted

Tailor your résumé to the job for which you're applying. Use keywords from the employer's job description to highlight your strengths.

- Monster.com
- MyFuture.com
- Resume-Now.com
- TheBalance.com
- TheMuse.com

Keep the résumé to one page, and tailor it to the specific job you want. For instance, if you're applying for a job as a ferry captain or deckhand, emphasize your boating experience. However, if you want to drive a school bus, the employer will be less interested in how much time you've spent cruising on a lake.

Choose what to include and what to omit according to what the employer wants. Emphasize examples of your personal qualities that workers need for the job. Your résumé should also include your education, previous employment, volunteer work, and personal interests and hobbies. Add any special training, certifications, or licenses you hold. (Or, attach photocopies of the items to your application.) Carefully read the job description. As you describe your qualifications, use keywords and phrases that mirror that description.

The order you present the information depends on the job and your situation. Put the most important items in the top one-third of the page, so a recruiter can quickly scan the document and see the ways you qualify. If you're strong on work experience, put that first. If you have little experience, put your education and training first.

Your contact information should have a professional tone. If your email address is something like PartyAnimal@xyz.com, create a new one using just your name: annjones@xyz.com. Record a professional sounding voice mail message on the phone you'll want potential employers to use to contact you. Be sure to visit your social media pages before employers see them. Delete party pics, as well as anything that reflects poorly on your character. (Better yet, don't post them in the first place!) Visiting applicants' social media sites is becoming standard procedure for employers. Some candidates have lost opportunities due to what employers saw there.

When you finish creating your document, run a spell-checking program in your word processing software. Then read the entire page word-for-word. Proofread. Proofread. Proofread. Then ask a trusted adult to proofread it again.

ON THE JOB HUNT

Finding openings for public transportation occupations is as easy as clicking a mouse. The first places to look are the websites of the agencies that operate the transit systems. Many of these agencies list job openings there. Other good places to search are websites for the local unions that represent these types of workers.

Several job listings appear on such other websites as the following:
- CareerBuilder.com
- Craigslist.org

(continued on the next page)

(continued from the previous page)

- Indeed.com
- Jobs.net
- JobsMonster.com
- TopUSAJobs.com
- Snagajob.com
- Unionjobs.com

You can also use free resources at public libraries and talk to drivers and operators of public transit vehicles. Ask if they know of any openings. Finally, attend job fairs in your area. A job fair is an event where representatives of many employers meet with job seekers. The representatives have information about the companies and agencies, current openings, work environment, and how to apply.

Let's Talk

If you're called in for an interview, prepare yourself. Visit the employer's official website. Read it thoroughly. Pay attention to any issues or problems with which the agency is dealing. You'll find that information in a section of the company's news releases, if one exists. Google the employer. Look for news articles, customer reviews, and any employee reviews concerning the agency. Jot down questions you can ask during the interview to show that you've done your research.

On the day of the interview, dress in neat, clean clothes that are appropriate for the job. You'll likely

Help Wanted

For an employment interview, dress for the job you want. Most transit workers wear uniforms, so business casual attire can replace a suit and tie.

wear a uniform on the job, but men don't need a formal suit and tie to apply. Women don't need expensive dresses. For public transportation job interviews, men should wear khakis or nice pants with a collared shirt. Women can wear business casual pants or dresses.

Make a practice run to the interview location a few days before at the same time you'll be traveling to the interview. Keep in mind schedules of any public transit you may use. Arrive ten to fifteen minutes early. If you get there earlier than that, wait a while before entering the building. You want to be prompt without appearing too eager.

When you're called in, smile, shake hands, and look the interviewer in the eye. Let the interviewer talk as much as possible. Ask questions about the job and the employer. However, avoid discussion of shifts, wages, benefits, or vacation time. You'll learn those answers when you're offered the job. Emphasize your desire to help the employer achieve its goals.

The interviewer will likely ask you about items on your résumé. Smile again. Answer truthfully and confidently, without exaggerating or appearing to brag. The interviewer may ask such questions as how you would handle a hypothetical situation or how you have handled a similar situation in real life. He or she may also ask where you see yourself in ten or fifteen years. The answer to this question will show how ambitious you are and whether you plan to work for the employer for a short time or the long haul.

At the end of the interview, ask for the job. Most applicants are too shy to do that, fearing they'll be turned down. However, hiring decisions are rarely

Help Wanted

As soon as possible after an interview, write a thank-you note or send a thank-you email to the interviewer or interviewers you met.

made at the first interview, so you're not likely to be rejected face-to-face. Go ahead and risk it. Many hiring managers are impressed by those who show they want the job. If you're not hired on the spot, ask when the employer will make a decision. Smile, shake hands, and express thanks for the interview.

After the interview, send a message of thanks. Add that you're interested in the opening. If you haven't heard anything within the time the interviewer told you, call and ask about the status of your application. If you get the job, congratulations! If not, thank the hiring manager. Stay positive. Apply somewhere else.

Glossary

ABLE SEAMAN An experienced merchant mariner deckhand.

AMERICAN SIGN LANGUAGE (ASL) An unspoken language that uses hand and finger gestures, movements, and facial expressions to convey meaning.

BOROUGH A division of a city.

CATENARY WIRE A system of overhead wires that provides electricity to trains and allows faster acceleration, lower noise levels, and reduced negative air quality effects.

COMMERCIAL DRIVER'S LICENSE (CDL) A driver's license required for bus drivers earned by passing written and driving tests.

COUPLING A method of connecting railcars.

DEAD MAN'S PEDAL An electrical switch that automatically activates if the operator of a train (or other vehicle or machine) loses control. If an operator dies, loses consciousness, or is physically removed from control, the train slows, idles, or stops.

EXTRA BOARD Commuter train engineers and conductors who work as temporary substitute workers.

HYDROPLANE To skid out of control on a film of water on a road's surface, causing loss of contact between a vehicle's tires and the road.

HYPOTHERMIA A medical condition of dangerously low body temperature.

INTERVIEW A face-to-face meeting between an applicant and a representative of the employer.

JOB FAIR An event where representatives of a large group of employers meet with job seekers.

LABOR UNION An organization of workers that serves to improve member benefits and working conditions through negotiations with employers concerning such issues as wages, hours, fringe benefits, and job security.

ORDINARY SEAMAN A new merchant mariner with little or no experience.

P ENDORSEMENT An additional certification on a commercial driver's license that shows that the driver is qualified to drive vehicles that hold at least sixteen passengers.

RÉSUMÉ A document that lists a job applicant's education, work experience, and other qualifications.

RIGHT OF WAY A legal right to pass along a specific route.

S ENDORSEMENT An additional certification on a commercial driver's license that shows that the driver is qualified to drive a school bus.

SENIORITY The time the worker has served on the job compared to other employees.

SIMULATOR A machine or piece of equipment used for training purposes that imitates the environment and other conditions of an actual event, such as operating a vehicle.

For More Information

American Public Transportation Association
1300 I Street NW, Suite 1200 East
Washington, DC 20005
(202) 496-4800
Website: http://www.apta.com
Facebook: @americanpublictransportationassociation
Twitter: @APTA_info
The American Public Transportation Association represents public organizations in the fields of bus, paratransit, light-rail, commuter rail, subways, waterborne passenger services, and high-speed rail. It works to improve public transportation and ensure its availability and accessibility in the United States.

Canadian Urban Transit Association
55 York Street, Suite 1401
Toronto, Ontario M5J 1R7
Canada
(416) 365-9800
Website: http://www.cutaactu.ca
Facebook: @CanadianTransit
Twitter: @canadiantransit
This association represents the public transit community in Canada. Its activities include conferences, training, public affairs, awards, exhibitions, technical services, research, statistics and government relations.

Community Transportation Association of America (CTTA)
1341 G Street, NW
Suite 250
Washington, DC 20005
(800) 891-0590

Website: http://web1.ctaa.org/webmodules/webarticles/anmviewer.asp?a=23&z=2

CTTA members provide safe, affordable, and reliable transportation regardless of age, ability, geography, or income. They are dedicated to their passengers and their communities.

Federal Motor Carrier Safety Administration (FMCSA)
US Department of Transportation
1200 New Jersey Avenue SE
Washington, DC 20590
(800) 832-5660
Website: https://www.fmcsa.dot.gov

The FMCSA is the part of the US Department of Transportation that works to prevent commercial motor vehicle–related fatalities and injuries. It enforces safety regulations and works to strengthen safety information systems and equipment and operating standards.

Federal Railroad Administration
1200 New Jersey Avenue SE
Washington, DC 20590
Website: https://www.fra.dot.gov/Page/P0001
Facebook and Twitter: @USDOTFRA

The Federal Railroad Administration is part of the US Department of Transportation. It enforces rail safety regulations, administers railroad assistance programs, and conducts research to improve safety. It also promotes national rail transportation policy.

National School Transportation Association (NSTA)
623 North Broad Street
Lansdale, PA 19446

For More Information

(703) 684-3200
Website: http://www.yellowbuses.org
Facebook: @nsta1
Twitter: @nstayellowbuses
NSTA members seek to provide safe, secure, environmentally responsible, and cost-effective school bus transportation in the United States. The association also offers education, community involvement, and industry advocacy.

Passenger Vessel Association
103 Oronoco Street, Suite 200
Alexandria, VA 22314
(800) 807-8360
Website: http://www.passengervessel.com
The Passenger Vessel Association promotes the interests of US passenger vessel owners and operators. It promotes safety for passengers and crew, as well as business and regulatory issues.

Transportation Association of Canada
401 - 1111 Prince of Wales Drive
Ottawa, ON K2C 3T2
Canada
(613) 736-1350
Website: http://www.tac-atc.ca
Facebook: @tac2014atc
The Transportation Association of Canada promotes safe, secure, efficient, effective, and environmentally and financially sustainable transportation services in Canada.

US Coast Guard National Maritime Center
100 Forbes Drive
Martinsburg, WV 25404-7120

(888) 427-5662
Website: http://www.dco.uscg.mil/Our-Organization Assistant-Commandant-for-Prevention-Policy-CG 5P/National-Maritime-Center-NMC/Contact
Facebook: @uscoastguard
Twitter: @uscg
The US Coast Guard National Maritime Center is a credentialing program for US mariners. Its goal is to ensure a safe, economically viable, and environmentally sound marine transport system.

For Further Reading

Abdallah, Thomas. *Sustainable Mass Transit: Challenges and Opportunities*. Amsterdam, Netherlands: Elsevier, 2017.

Angulo, Roberto. *Getting Your First Job for Dummies*. Hoboken, NJ: John Wiley & Sons, 2017.

Bookstein, Ezra, and Jeremy Workman. *One-Track Mind: Drawing the New York Subway*. New York: Princeton Architectural Press, 2018.

CDL Exam Secrets Test Prep Team. *CDL Exam Secrets - CDL Practice Tests & All CDL Endorsements Study Guide: CDL Test Review for the Commercial Driver's License.* Beaumont, TX: Mometrix Media, 2013.

Cheney, Frank, and Anthony M. Sammarco. *Boston in Motion*. Charleston, SC: Arcadia Publishing, 1999.

Cheney, Frank, and Anthony M. Sammarco. *Trolleys Under the Hub* (Images of America). Charleston, SC: Arcadia Publishing, 1997.

Clarke, Thomas Curtis. *The American Railway: Its Construction, Development, Management, and Trains*. New York: Skyhorse Publishing, 2012.

Davis, Katrinell M. *Hard Work Is Not Enough: Gender and Racial Inequality in an Urban Workspace.* Chapel Hill: University of North Carolina Press, 2016.

Elder, Andrew, and Jeremy C. Fox. *Boston's Orange Line* (Images of Rail). Charleston, SC: Arcadia Publishing, 2013.

FitzGerald, Warren. *All in the Same Boat: The Untold Story of the British Ferry Crew Who Helped Win the Falklands War*. London, England: John Blake, 2016.

Huff, Stephen. *Bus Driver, Bus Driver: Violence Redeeming Collected Short Stories 2009–2011*. League City, TX: Capital Ideations, 2016.

Ingersoll-Sergeant Drill Company. *Driving the New York Subway: March 24, 1900–October 27, 1904*. London, England: Forgotten Books, 2017.

Kelly, John. *Chicago Postwar Passenger and Commuter Trains.* Hudson, WI: Enthusiast Publishing, 2012.

McKendry, Joe. *Beneath the Streets of Boston: Building America's First Subway.* Jaffrey, NH: David R. Godine, 2005.

Most, Doug. *The Race Underground: Boston, New York, and the Incredible Rivalry That Built America's First Subway.* New York, NY: St. Martin's Press, 2014.

National Park Service. *The Ferry Boat, Ellis Island: Transport to Hope.* Washington, DC: BiblioGov, 2012.

Trimble, Paul C., and William Knorp. *Ferries on San Francisco Bay.* Charleston, SC: Arcadia Publishing, 2007.

Yate, Martin. *Knock 'em Dead: Job Interview: How to Turn Job Interviews into Job Offers.* Avon, MA: Adams Media, 2012.

Yate, Martin. *Knock 'em Dead: The Ultimate Job Search Guide.* Avon, MA: Adams Media, 2017.

Bibliography

Amalgamated Transit Union. "Our Work." Retrieved February 13, 2018. https://www.atu.org/work/school.

Borysek, Marilyn. "6 Tips for Writing an Effective Resume." ASME, March 2011. https://www.asme.org/career-education/articles/job-hunting/6-tips-for-writing-an-effective-resume.

Bureau of Labor Statistics. *Occupational Outlook Handbook.* US Department of Labor. Retrieved February 13, 2018. https://www.bls.gov.

Citrano, Virginia. "Why Vincent Lombardi Plays Himself in 'Sully.'" MyVeronaNJ.com, September 9, 2016. http://www.myveronanj.com/2016/09/19/vincent-lombardi-plays-sully.

DMV.org. "CDL Endorsements." Retrieved February 13, 2018. https://www.dmv.org/cdl/passenger-school-bus-endorsement.php.

Donnelly, Ally. "Still Waiting: MBTA Commuters Frustrated by Lack of Improvement." NBCBoston.com, March 9, 2017. https://www.nbcboston.com/news/local/MBTA-investments-investigation-415790143.html.

Experis. "20 Tips for Great Job Interviews." Experis, April 12, 2018. https://www.experisjobs.us/exp_us/en/career-advice/20-tips-job-interviews.htm.

Fenske, Sarah. "Metro Light Rail Operators Don't Have a Contract—Just Grueling Schedules and Smelly Passengers." *Phoenix New Times*, April 23, 2009. http://www.phoenixnewtimes.com/news/metro-light-rail-operators-dont-have-a-contract-just-grueling-schedules-and-smelly-passengers-6431148.

Forgey, Pat. "Alaska 'bridge to nowhere' plan is no more as state chooses ferry for Ketchikan." *Alaska*

Daily News, September 28, 2016. https://www.adn.com/alaska-news/article/bridge-nowhere-no-more-dot-choses-ferry-ketchikan/2015/10/23.

GuinnessWorldRecords.com. "Longest Career as a Bus Driver." Retrieved February 12, 2018. http://www.guinnessworldrecords.com/world-records/longest-career-as-a-bus-driver.

Haller, Scott. "MBTA Commuter Rail Only System in Country in Decline." PioneerInstitute.com, February 18, 2015. https://pioneerinstitute.org/blog/mbta-commuter-rail-only-system-in-country-in-decline-over-the-last-decade.

Hanna, Jason, and Doug Criss. "The deadliest US commuter train crashes in the past two decades." CNN.com, February 4, 2018. https://www.cnn.com/2016/09/29/us/us-commuter-train-wreck-history-trnd/index.html.

McCarthy, Niall. "The U.S. Cities with the Most Homeless People." Statista.com, January 26, 2018. https://www.statista.com/chart/6949/the-us-cities-with-the-most-homeless-people.

MyVesselLogs.com. "The U.S. Coast Guard Regulations for Ferryboats." Retrieved February 13, 2018. http://www.myvessellogs.com/blog/The-U-S-Coast-Guard-s-Regulations-for-Ferryboats.

O-Net online. "Ship and Boat Captains." Retrieved February 13, 2018. https://www.onetonline.org/link/summary/53-5021.01.

Rockport Institute. "How to Write a Masterpiece of a Resume." Rockport Institute. Retrieved April 6, 2018. https://rockportinstitute.com/resources/how-to-write-a-masterpiece-of-a-resume.

Severt, Natalie. "42 Amazing Resume Tips That You Can Use in 30 Minutes." UpToWork.com, February

Bibliography

6, 2018. https://uptowork.com/blog/resume-tips.

Staten Island Ferry.com. "Staten Island Ferry." Retrieved February 15, 2018. http://www.siferry.com.

Stimson, Robin. "Siemens rail business helps set Guinness World Record in San Diego." Siemens, November 5, 2014. http://news.usa.siemens.biz/blog/mobility/siemens-rail-business-helps-set-guinness-world-record-san-diego.

U.S. News & World Report. "Bus Driver." *U.S. News & World Report*. Retrieved May 5, 2018. https://money.usnews.com/careers/best-jobs/bus-driver.

Whaley, Monte. "RTD says $1.5 million simulator will help light-rail training." *Denver Post*, April 27, 2016. https://www.denverpost.com/2014/04/20/rtd-says-1-5-million-simulator-will-help-light-rail-training.

Wortman, Marc. *Public Transportation: On the Move*. New York: Harper Design, 2005.

Index

A
AnsaldoBreda cars, 34

B
Bay Area Rapid Transit (BART), 33–34
Boeing Vertol cars, 34

C
careers, 6
  duties, 6
  schedules, 6
certifications, 6, 54, 56
Class B commercial driver's license (CDL), 15
commuter rail, 4, 19, 20, 28
  benefits of, 4, 19, 20
  catenary wire, 20
  employment, 20, 21, 24, 27, 29
  engines, 20, 22
  service areas, 4, 20
  target market, 20
  trains, 4, 19, 20, 22
conductors, 20–21
  age requirement, 24
certification, 24
  education, 24, 25–26
  job outlook, 29
  responsibilities, 21–22
  schedule, 21
  skills, 24, 25
  technology, 24
  training, 24–25, 26

D
dead man's pedal, 33
disabled people, 6, 9, 12, 53

E
education, 6, 52, 53
elevated trains, 4, 30
  track, 30
equipment maintenance, 6

F
Federal Railroad Administration, 24, 26
ferries, 4–5, 43–44, 47
  passengers, 5, 43, 47
  vehicles, 5, 43
ferry captains, 43, 45, 46
  licensure, 49
  responsibilities, 45
  skills, 45
ferry deckhands, 43, 46, 49
  able seaman, 46, 50
  advancement, 50
  credentials, 49
  education, 49
  ordinary seaman, 46, 50
  responsibilities, 46
  skills, 46, 49
  training, 49
Fisher, Carl, 10

G
Guinness World Records, 10, 37

Index

H

hearing abilities, 6, 14, 24, 26, 49
homeless people, 13–14

J

job search, 52, 56, 58, 59–60, 64
  interview, 52, 60, 62, 64
  résumé, 52, 56, 58–59

L

licenses, 6, 54, 56
light-rail, 4, 30, 33
  benefits of, 30
  history of, 33–34
light-rail operators, 32, 36–37
  characteristics, 37
  education, 36
  job outlook, 40
  responsibilities, 32, 33
  schedule, 32, 39
  skills, 36–37, 38
  training, 38
light-rail systems, 34, 35–36
  C-Train (Calgary, Alberta, Canada), 36
  MetroLink (St. Louis, MO), 36
  Metropolitan Area Express (Portland, OR), 36
  Muni Metro (San Francisco, CA), 34, 35
  Regional Transportation District (RTD) (Denver, Colorado), 39
  Sacramento Regional Transit District System (Sacramento, CA), 36
  San Diego Trolley (San Diego, CA), 36
locomotive engineers, 20, 21
  age requirement, 24, 26
  certification, 26, 27
  education, 24
  job outlook, 29
  responsibilities, 22
  schedule, 21
  skills, 24, 27
  technology, 24
  training, 26–27
locomotive firers, 29
Lombardi, Vincent "Vinny," 41–43

M

Massachusetts Bay Transportation Authority (MBTA), 28
Merchant Mariner Credential, 49, 50
merchant mariners, 43, 50, 51
  job outlook, 51
"Miracle on the Hudson," 42
  Sully, 43

N

National Academy of Railroad Sciences, 26
National Transportation Safety Board, 23

77

O

on-the-job training, 6, 15, 26, 38, 49

P

passenger (P) endorsement, 15–16, 17
personal qualities, 6
positive train control (PTC), 23

R

railroad simulators, 38–39
Rail Safety Improvement Act of 2008, 23
right of way, 30, 35, 38

S

safety, 6, 9, 11, 17, 21–22, 23, 28, 39, 45, 49
  Chatsworth accident, 23
  Santa Clara County Valley Transit Authority, 13, 14
  Route 22, 13
school bus drivers, 7, 8, 9, 10, 11, 12, 17
  job outlook, 18
  responsibilities, 8, 9–10
  skills, 9, 10, 18
  training, 8
school bus (S) endorsement, 17
school buses, 4, 7
  cost to districts, 8
  safety of, 12
  seniority, 21, 39
  students, 8, 12
Siemens S200 class cars, 34–35
skills, 6, 14, 24, 36–37, 49, 52, 53, 54
  communication, 6, 52, 53, 54
  customer service, 6, 14, 24, 37, 49, 54
  decision-making, 6, 14, 24, 36
  observation, 6, 14
  technology, 6, 12, 52
Staten Island Ferry, 47, 48
  history, 47, 48
  Manhattan, 48
  Northfield, 48
streetcar operators, 32, 36–37
  characteristics, 37
  education, 36
  responsibilities, 32
  skills, 36–37, 38
  training, 38
streetcars, 4, 30, 36, 37
  KC Streetcar Project, 36
  Siemens S70, 37
  track, 30, 36
subways, 4, 30

T

texting, 23
transit buses, 4, 7, 8, 11

Index

passengers, 11
reliability, 4, 11
transit bus drivers, 7, 11–12, 14, 15, 18
 age requirement, 14
 certification, 15
 characteristics, 14
 education, 14, 15
 health, 14
 job outlook, 18
 licensure, 15
 responsibilities, 11–12
 schedule, 11, 18
 skills, 12, 14, 18
 training, 14, 15
Transportation Worker Identification Credential, 49
trolleys, 4, 30

U

unions, 8, 27, 39, 50
 Amalgamated Transit Union (ATU), 8, 11, 12, 27, 39–40, 50
 American Maritime Officers, 51
 Brotherhood of Locomotive Engineers and Trainmen, 27
 Commuter Rail Employees Union, 27
 Inland Boatmen's Union, 51
 International Organization of Masters, Mates & Pilots, 51
 Maritime Union, 51
 Sailors' Union of the Pacific, 51
 Seafarers International Union, 51
 Teamster Union, 8
 Transport Workers Union, 8
 United Transportation Union, 27
US Bureau of Labor Statistics, 18, 52
US Coast Guard, 42, 49
US Department of Labor, 12, 27, 29, 40, 51

V

vision, 6, 14, 24, 26, 49

About the Author

Mary-Lane Kamberg is a professional writer and the author of several books about careers from Rosen Publishing, including *A Career as a Plumber, Pipefitter, or Steamfitter*; *A Dream Job as a Sports Agent*; *Becoming a Database Administrator*; *Becoming a Systems Administrator*; *Getting a Job in the IT Industry*; *Working as a Mechanic in Your Community*; *Getting a Job in Law Enforcement, Security, and Corrections*; and *A Career as an Athletic Trainer*. She lives in Olathe, Kansas, and serves as coleader of the Kansas City Writers Group.

Photo Credits

Cover, p. 53 Monkey Business Images/Shutterstock.com; p. 3 and interior pages border Tateyama/Shutterstock.com; cover and interior pages (map) © iStockphoto.com/Pingebat; p. 5 Rorem/Shutterstock.com; p. 7 Monkeybusinessimages/iStock/Thinkstock; p. 9 FatCamera/E+/Getty Images; p. 11 MikeDotta/Shutterstock.com; pp. 16–17 Buzbuzzer/E+/Getty Images; p. 19 Wayhome Studio/Shutterstock.com; p. 21 Anna Jurkovska/Shutterstock.com; p. 25 Digital Vision/Photodisc/Thinkstock; p. 27 Patrice Latron/Corbis Documentary/Getty Images; p. 31 John Coletti/The Image Bank/Getty Images; p. 32 Mark Boster/Los Angeles Times/Getty Images; p. 35 © iStockphoto.com/Joe Potato; p. 40 Justin Sullivan/Getty Images; p. 41 © AP Images; p. 44 Kiev.Victor/Shutterstock.com; p. 48 Anthony Correia/Shutterstock.com; p. 50 Studio Barcelona/Shutterstock.com; p. 57 M-Imagephotography/iStock/Thinkstock; p. 61 Antoniodiaz/Shutterstock.com; p. 63 Digital Vision/Thinkstock.

Design and Layout: Nicole Russo-Duca; Editor: Bethany Bryan; Photo Researcher: Sherri Jackson